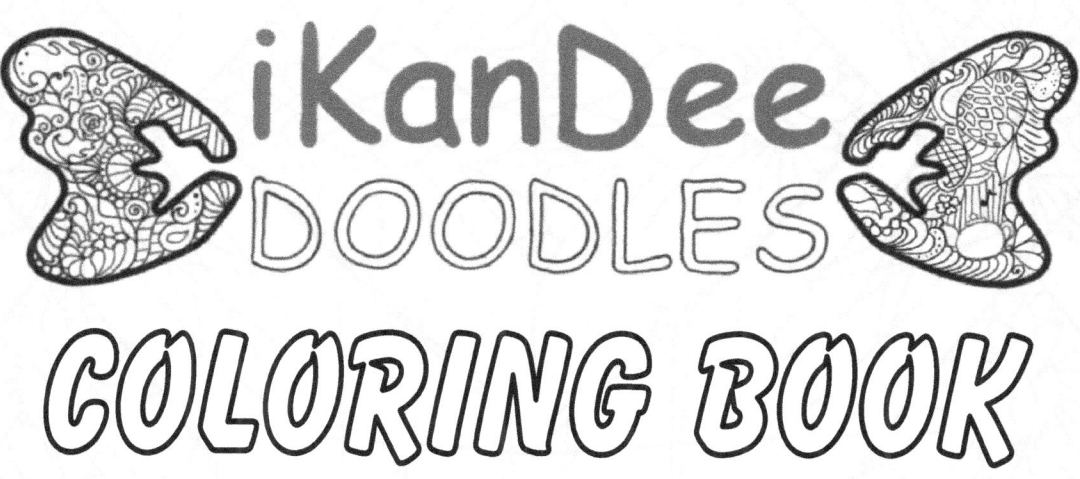

COLORING BOOK

THREE OF A KIND

Sheila D(ee)

"Relax & Have Fun"

iKanD(ee) Doodles
Coloring Book
Three Of A Kind

© 2020 Sheila D(ee)

All rights reserved.
No part of this book may be reproduced or transmitted in any form or by any means, electronic or mechanical, without permission in writing from the copyright owner and publisher.

DEDICATION:
Baby Girl, to the moon and back...

ACKNOWLEDGMENTS:
www.twitch.tv/thunderdomedru
DRU, thank you for shouting out my DOODLES!!!

If my Doodles by chance, put a smile on someone's face, that in itself, is an inspiration and I feel blessed.

~ BIG HUGGS ~
to my husband Dale,
my knight in shining armour,
truly, the love of my life.
~~~~~~~~~~~~~~~~~~~~~~~

CREDITS:
Book Cover is a photo of an iKanD(ee) Hand Dyed Fabric

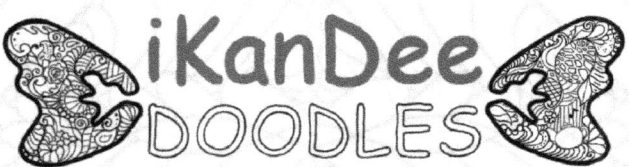

"Give Away A Smile... The Rewards Are Endless"

Coloring...
creative

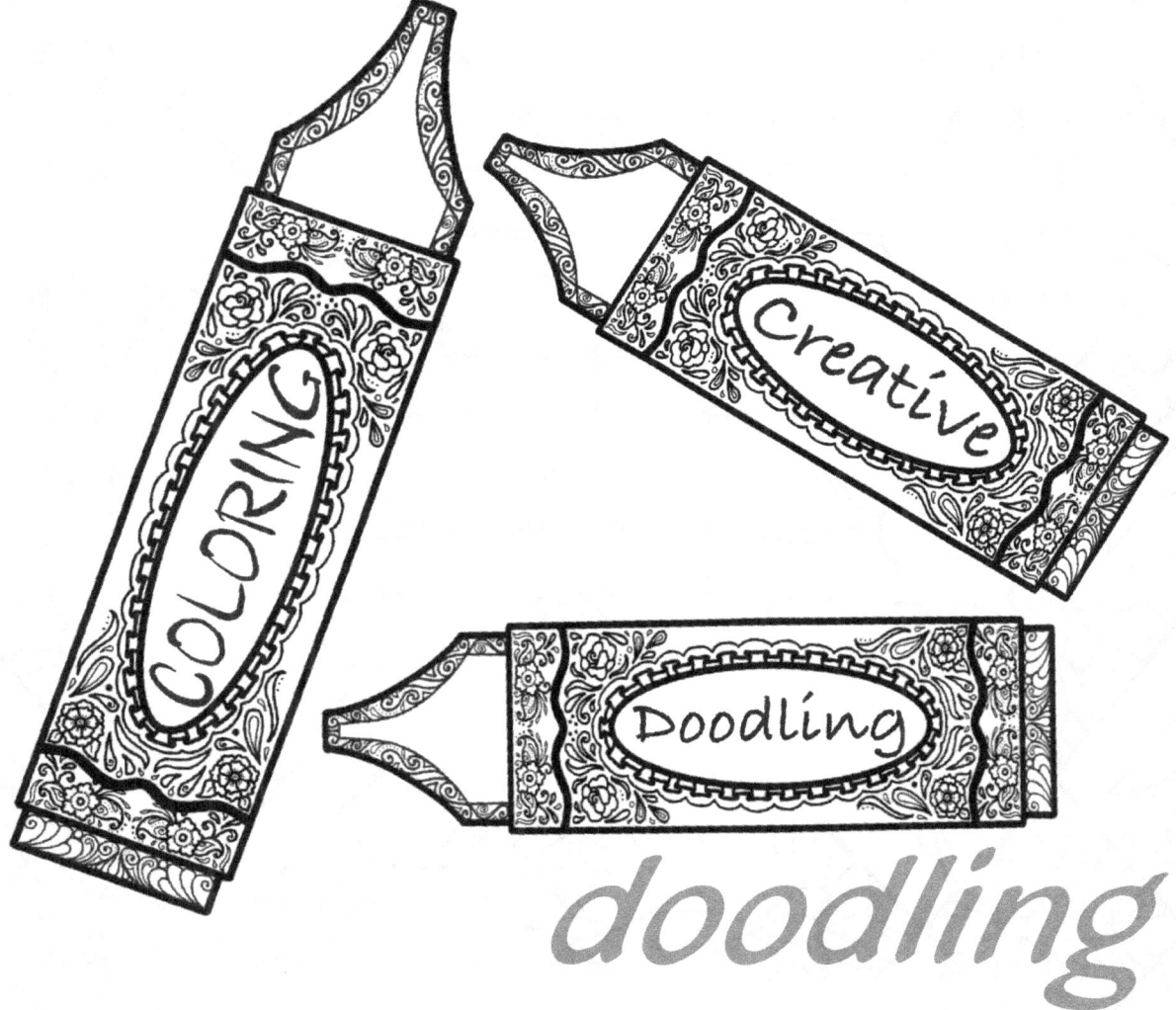

doodling

This Coloring Book Belongs To

_____

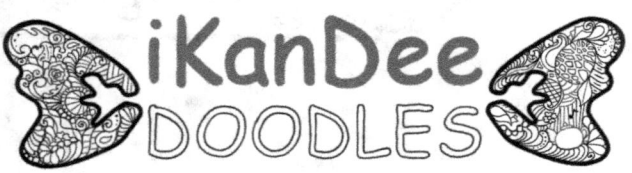

"Three Wise Monkeys"

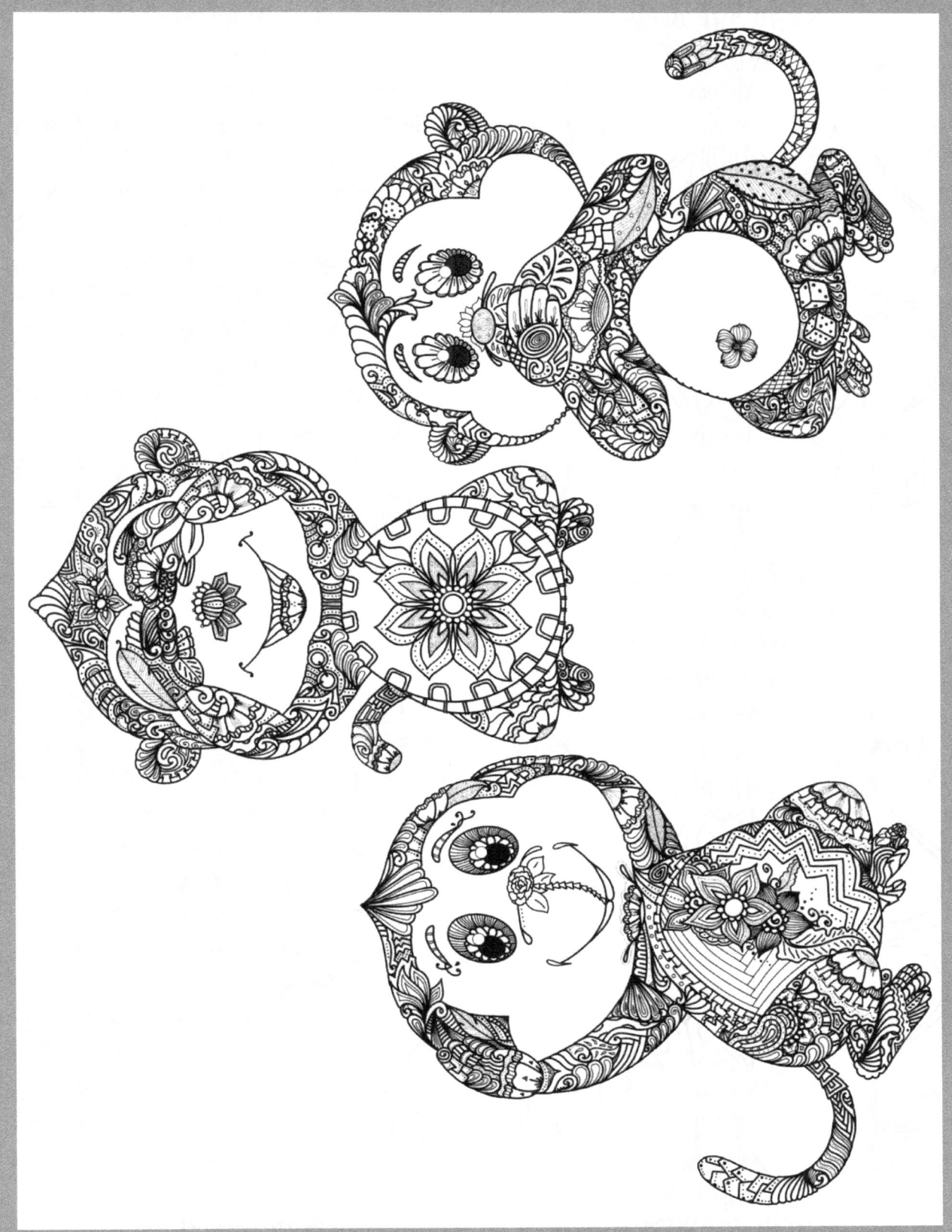

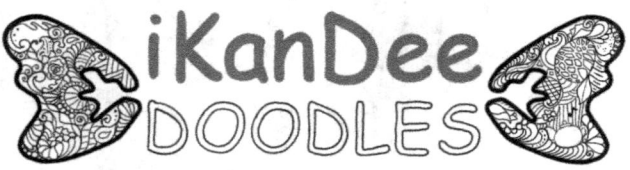

"See No Evil"

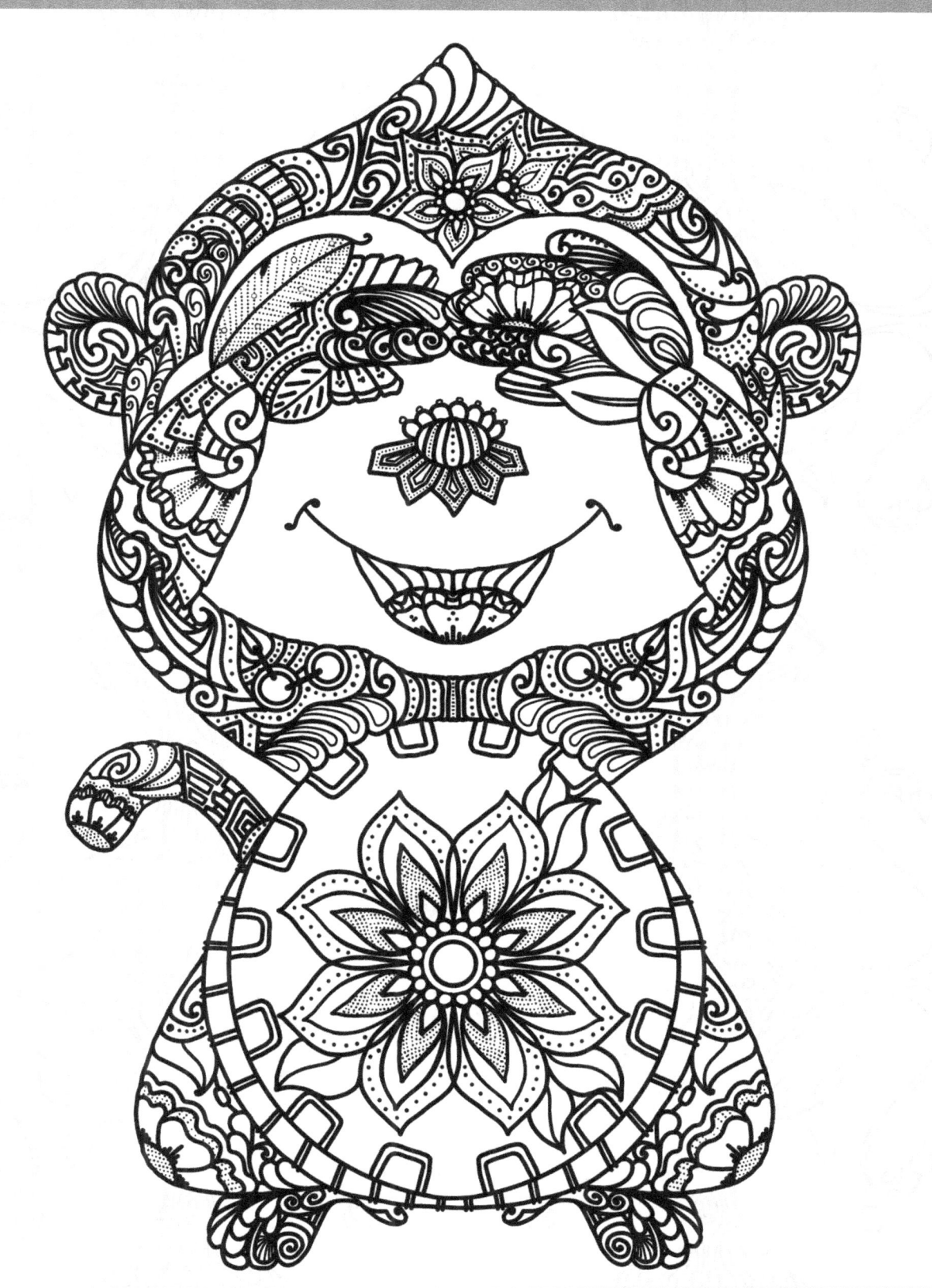

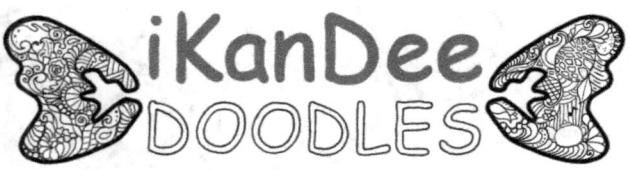

"Hear No Evil"

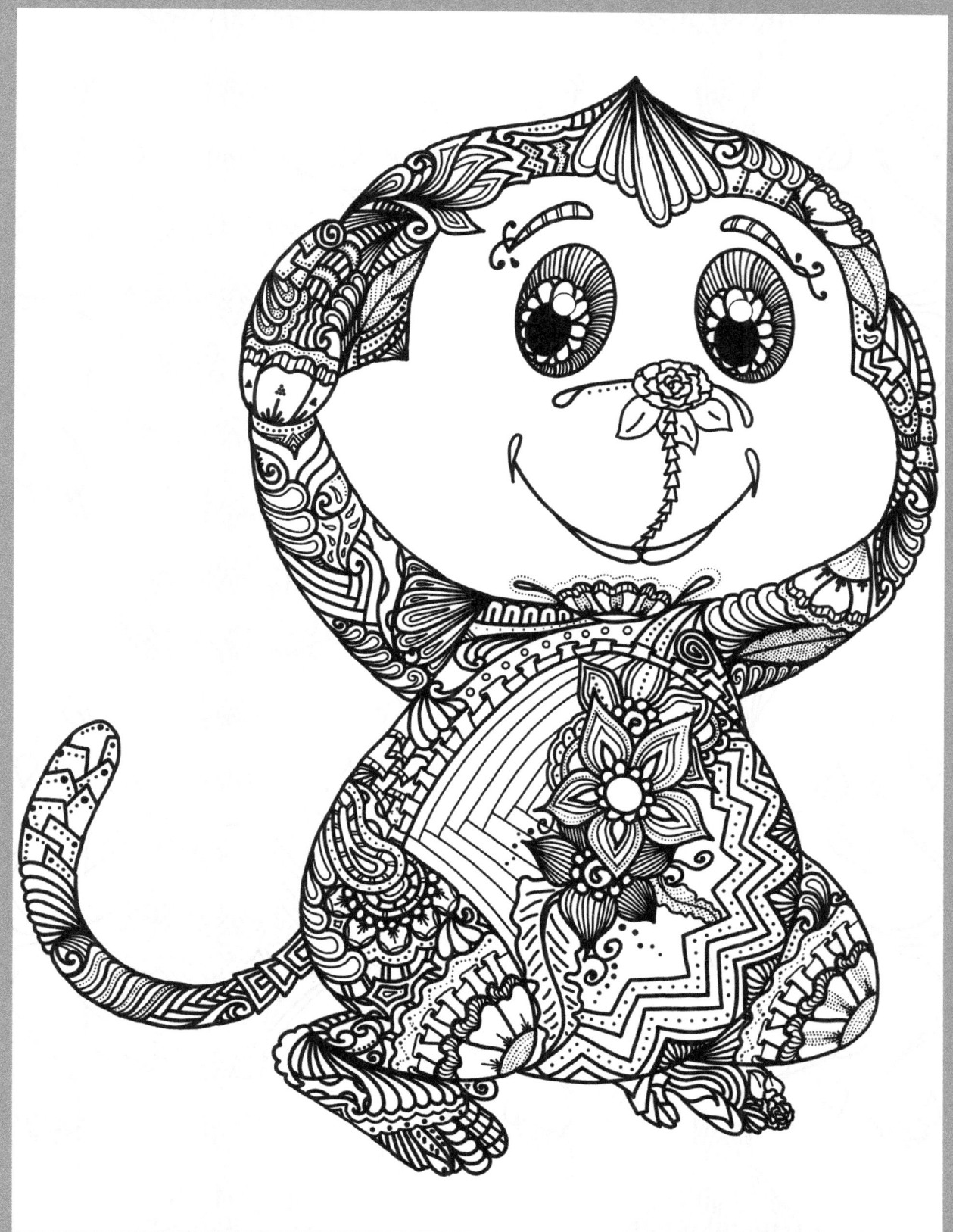

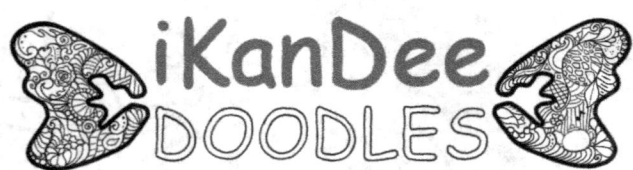

"Speak No Evil"

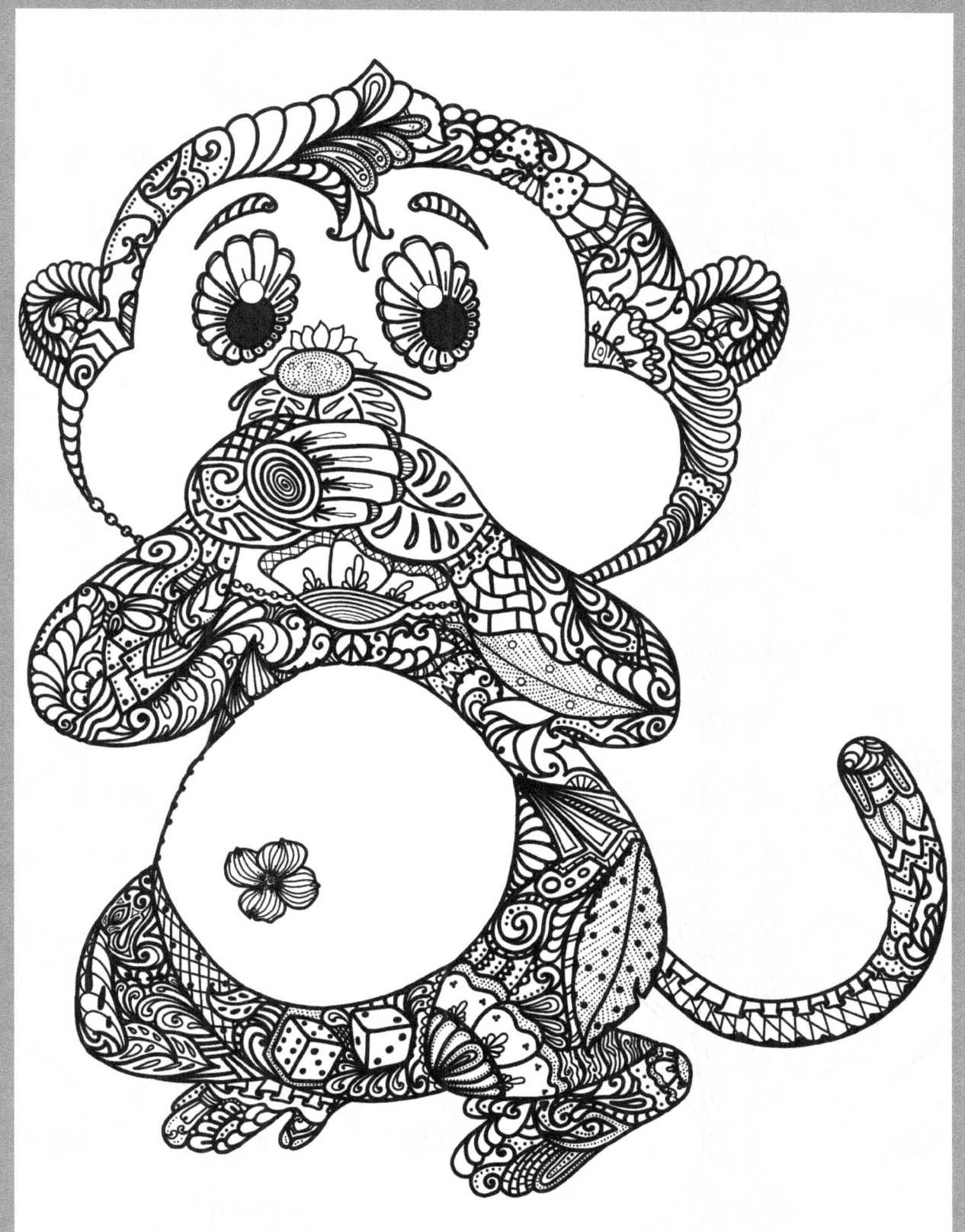

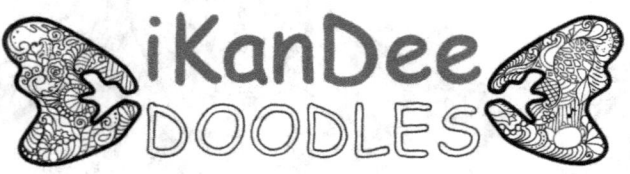

"Three Little Pigs"

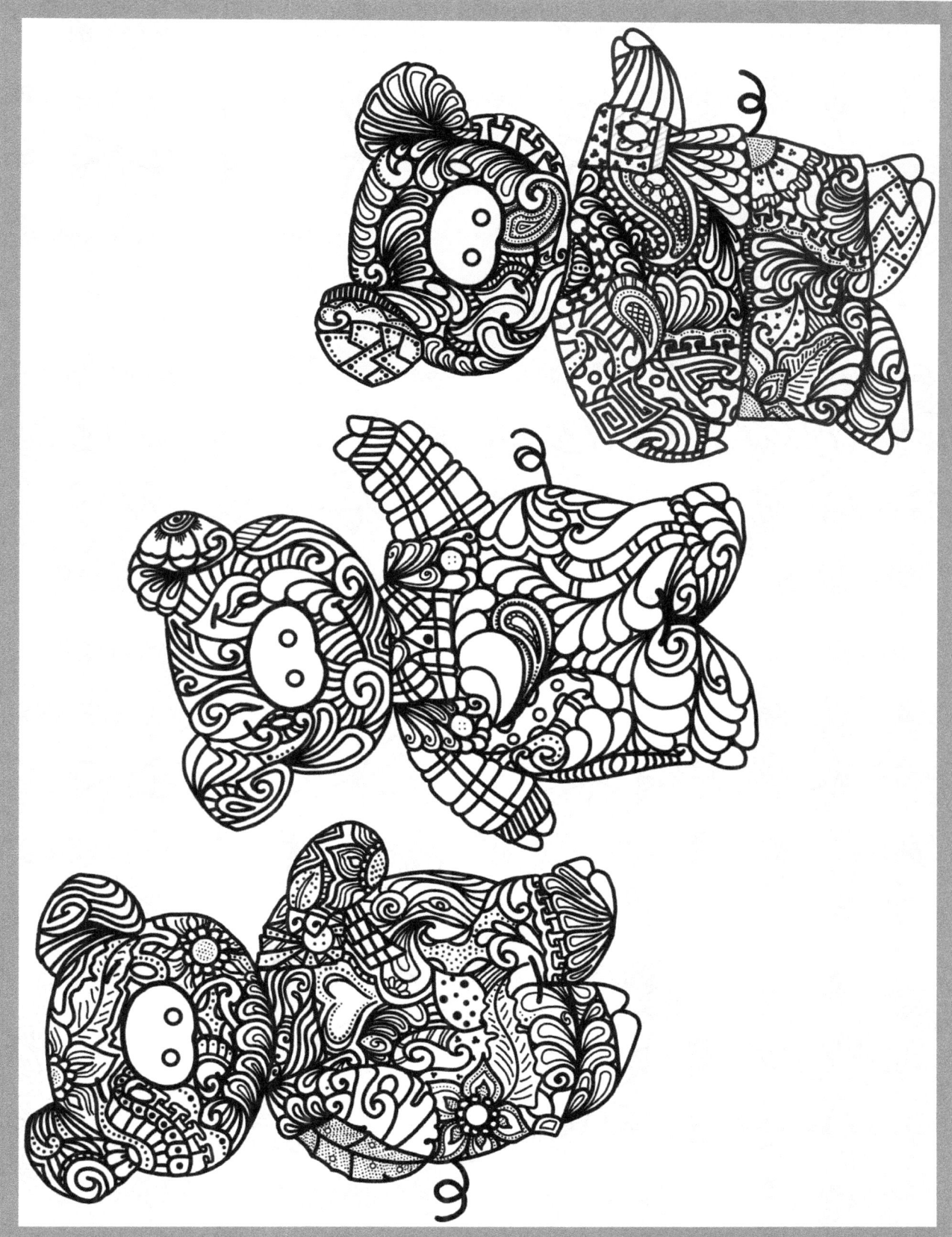

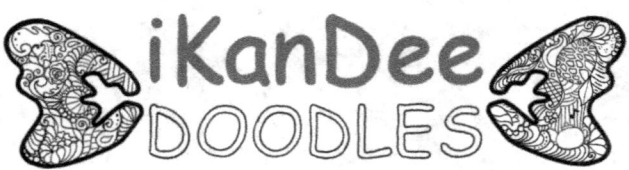

"Straw Piggy"

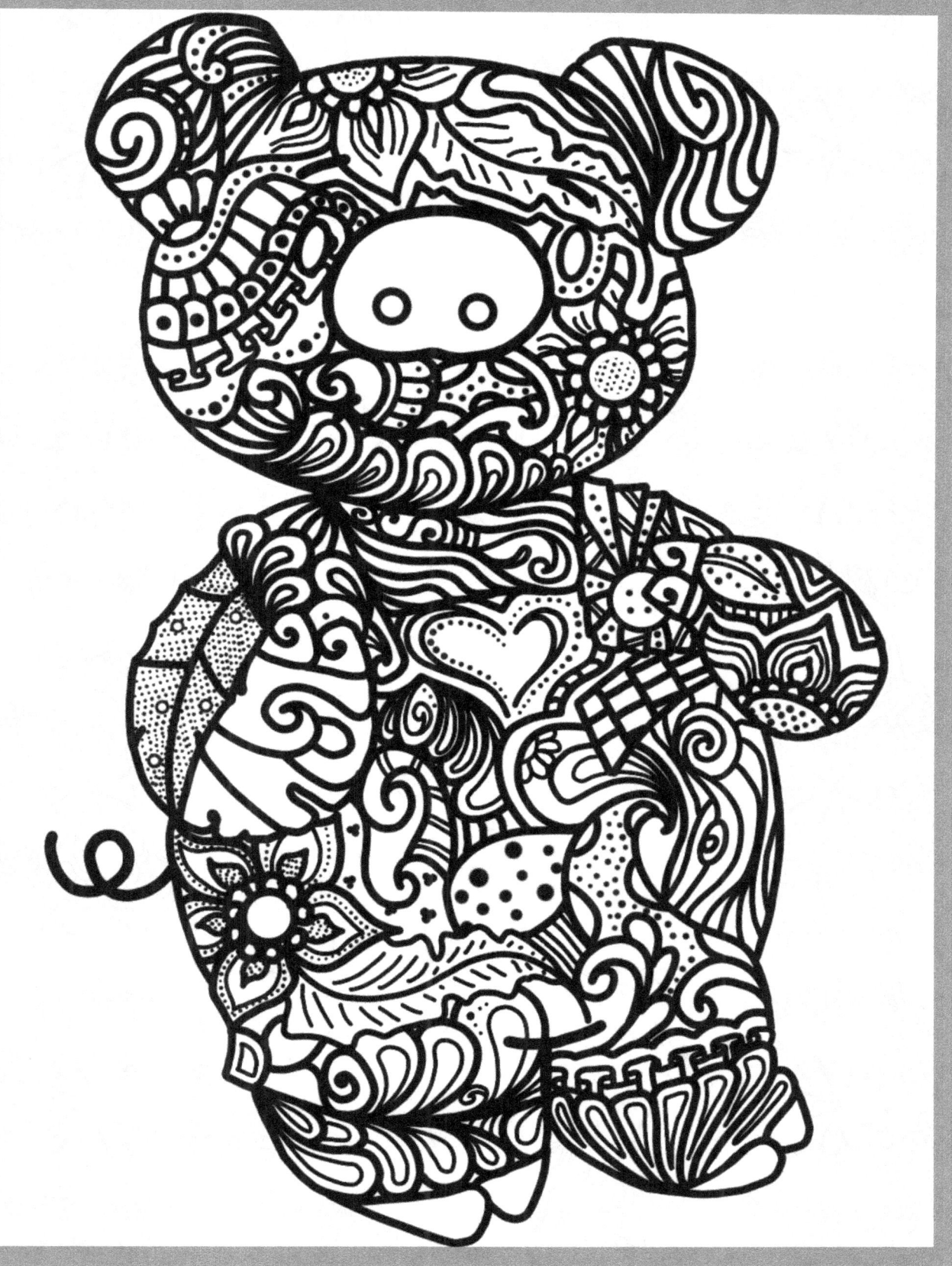

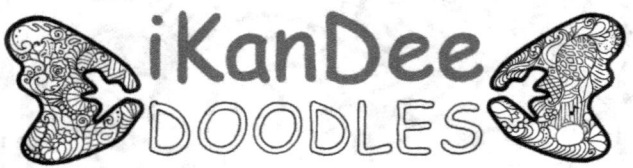

"Wood Piggy"

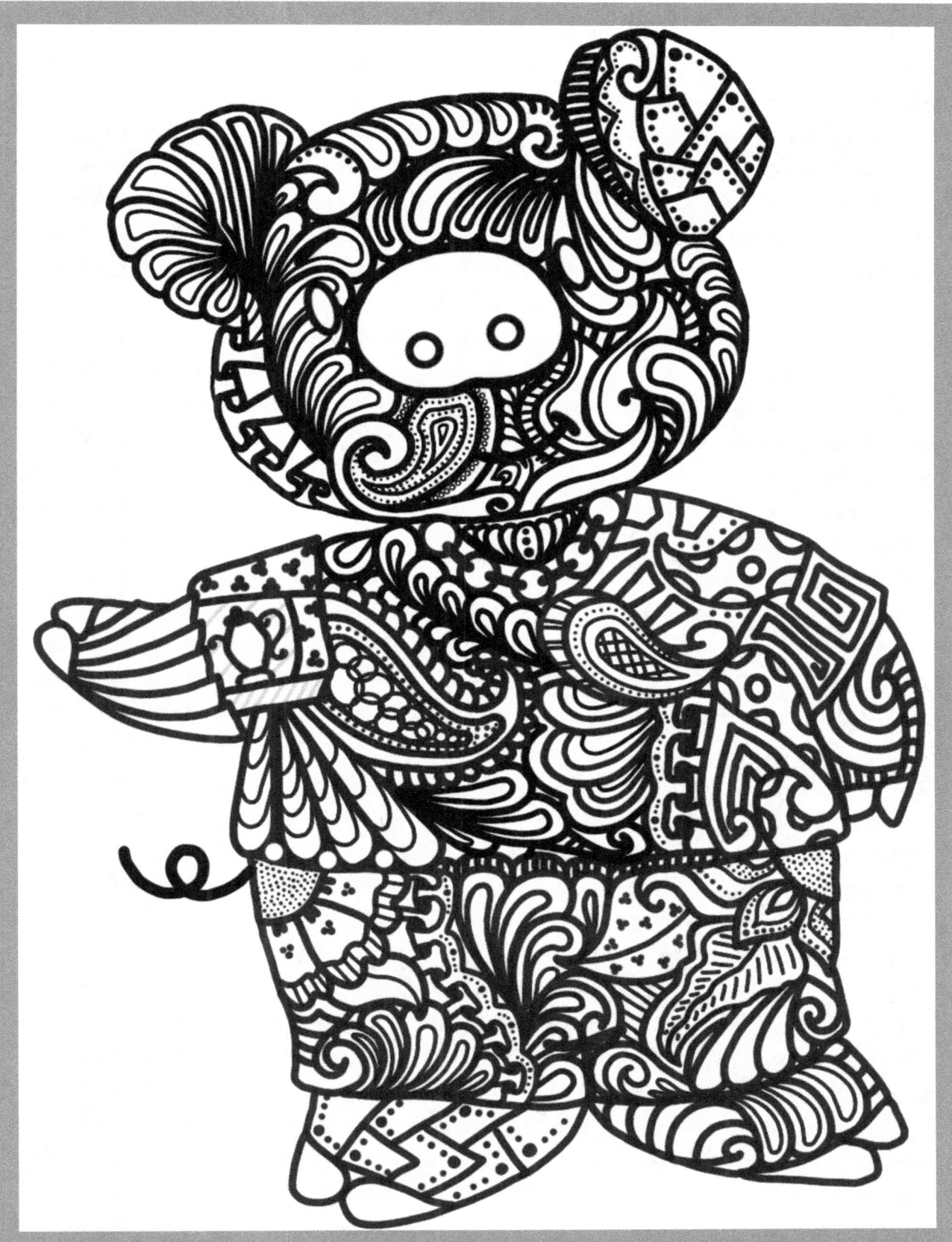

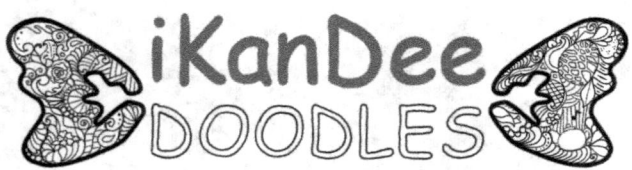

"Brick Piggy"

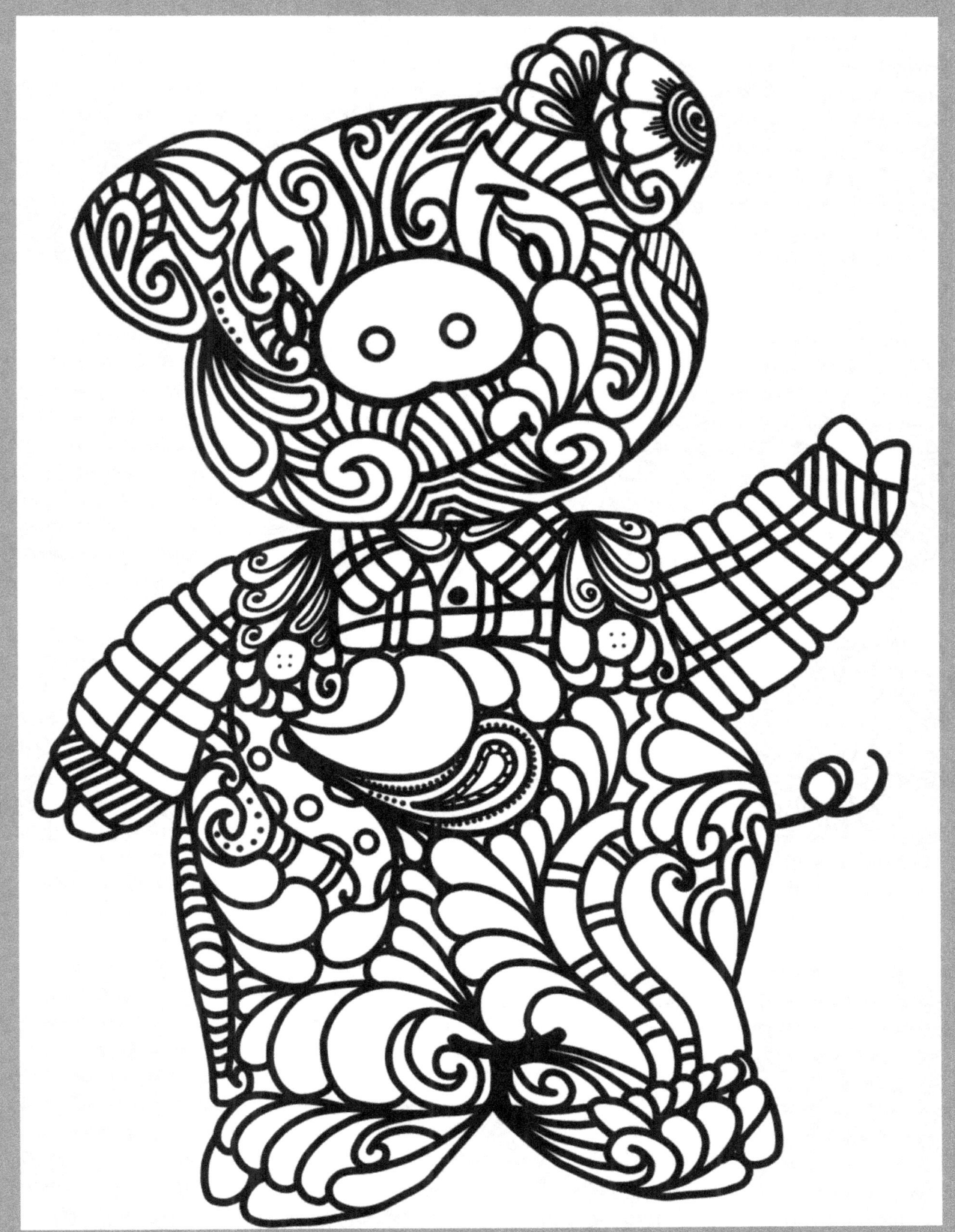

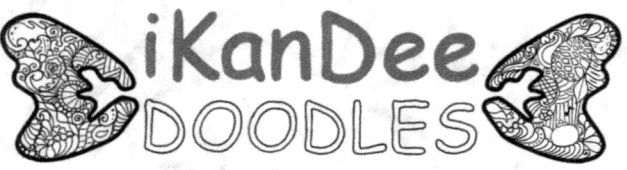

"Three Amigos"

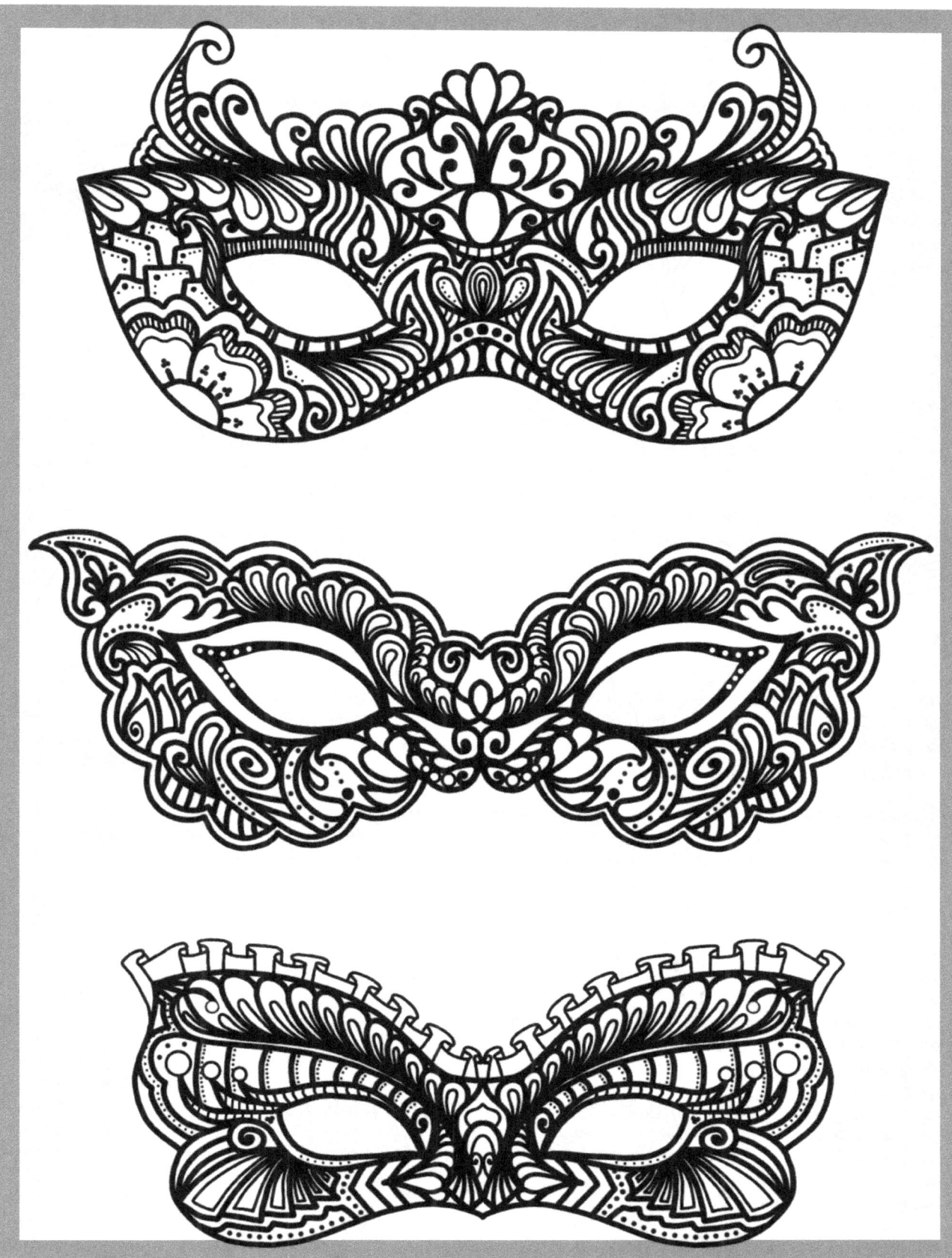

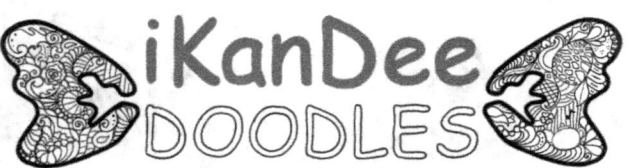

"Once"

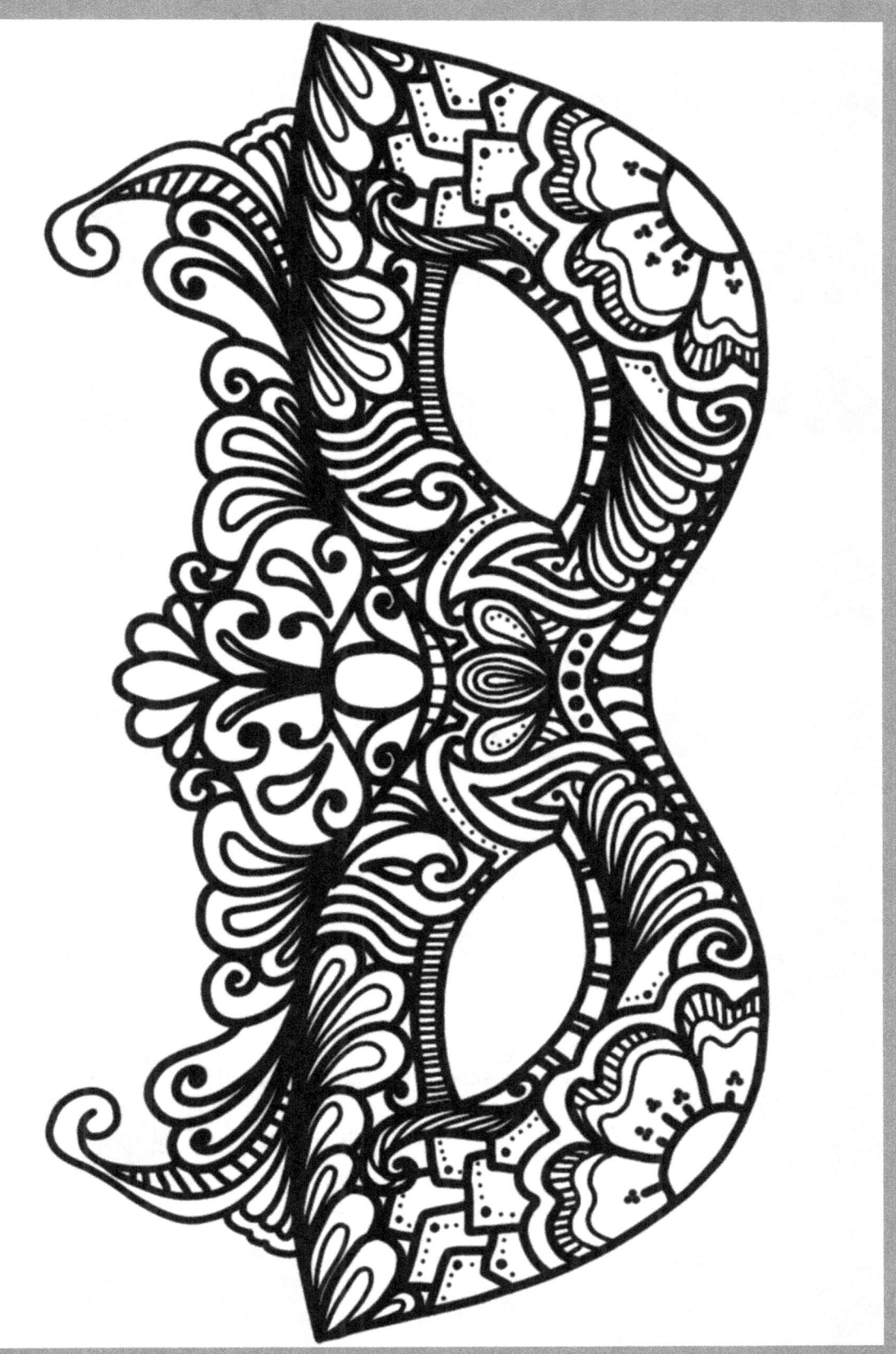

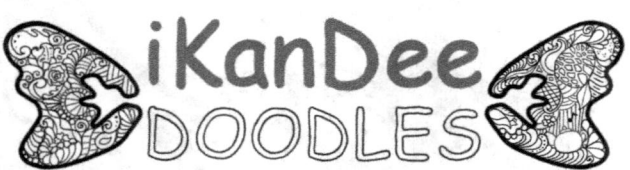

"Twice"

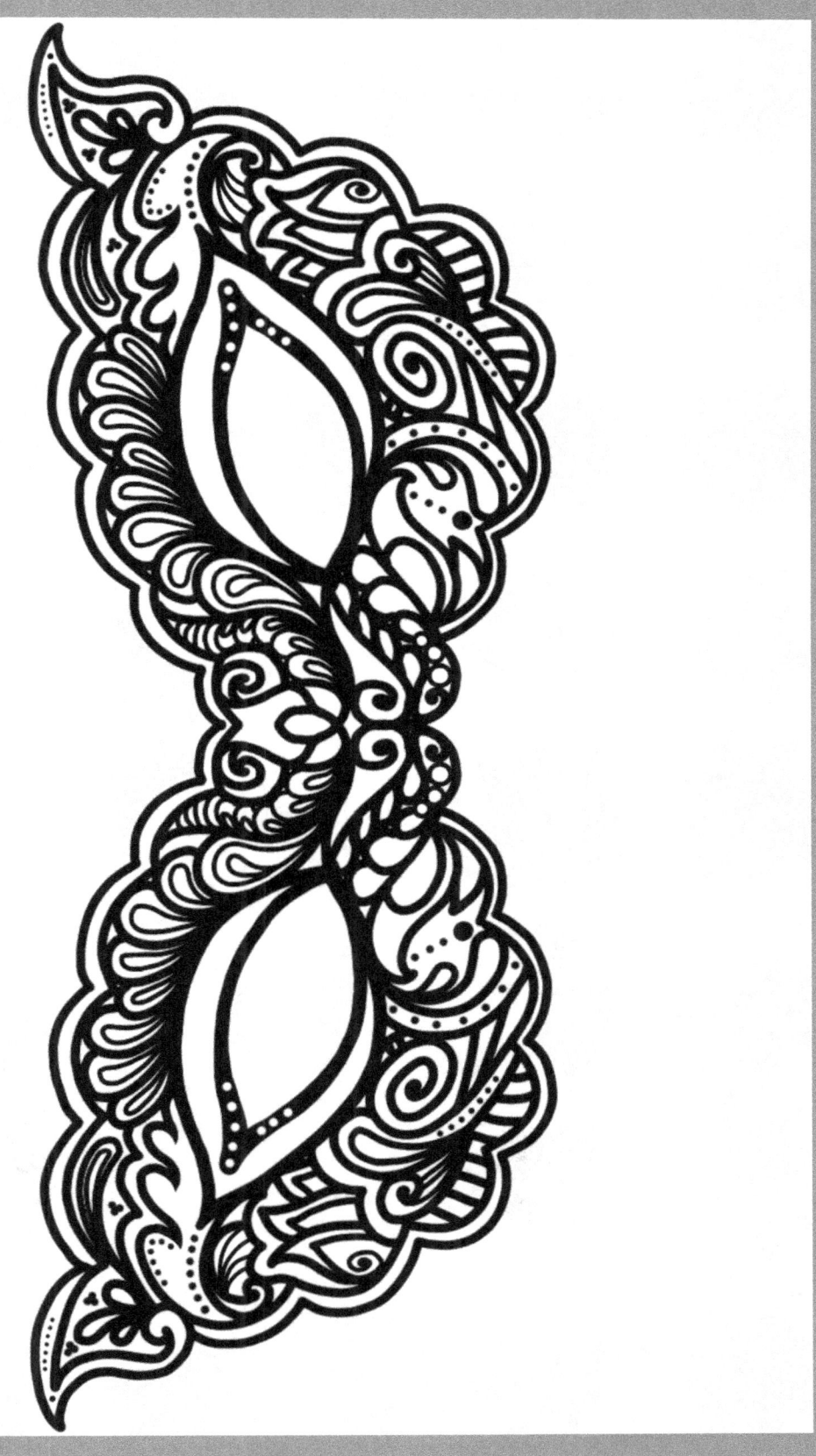

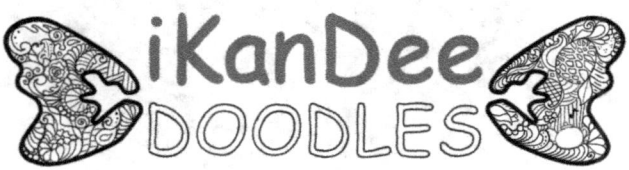

"Thrice"

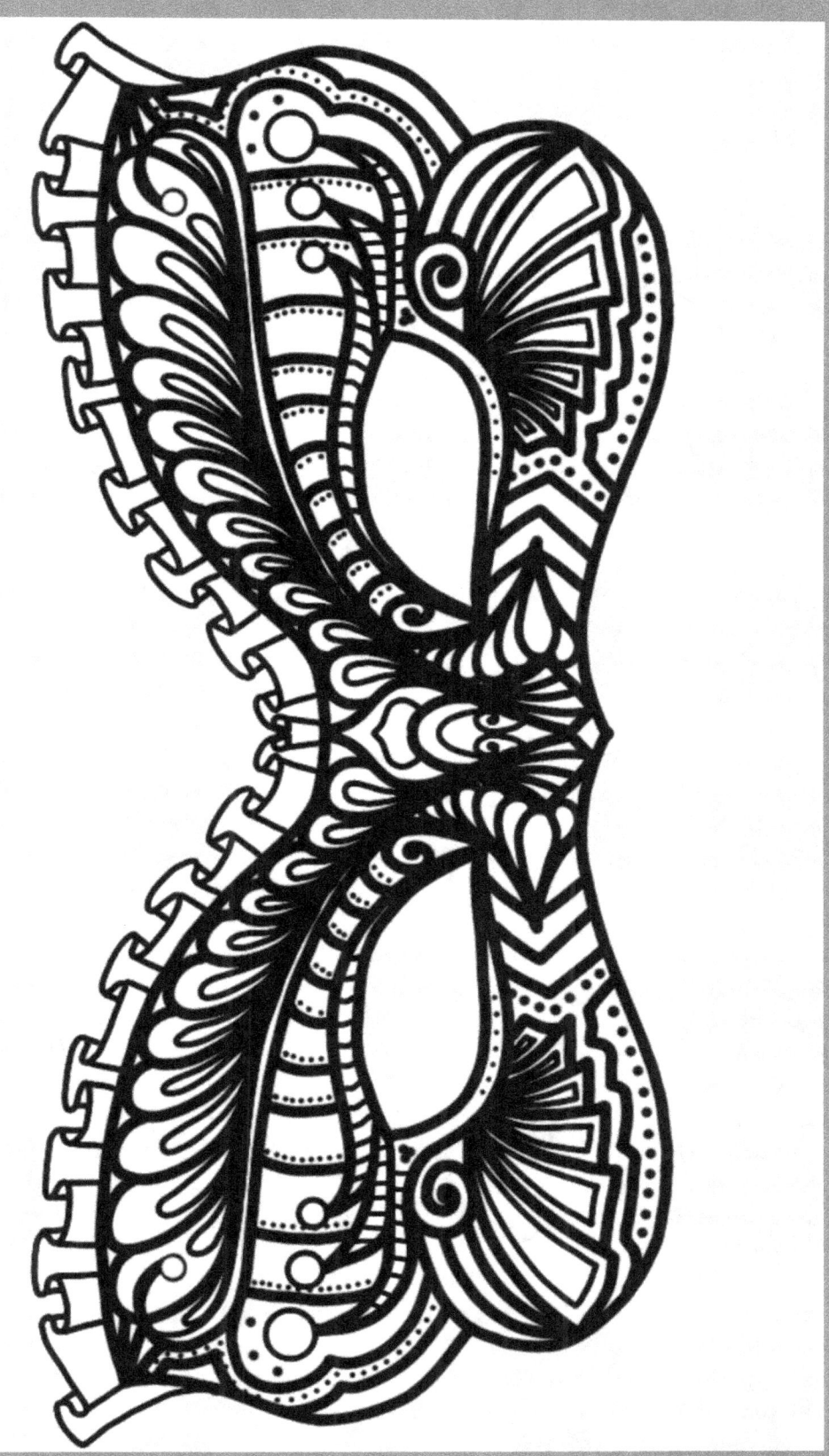

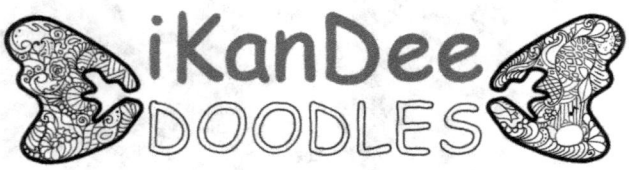

"Three Musketeers"

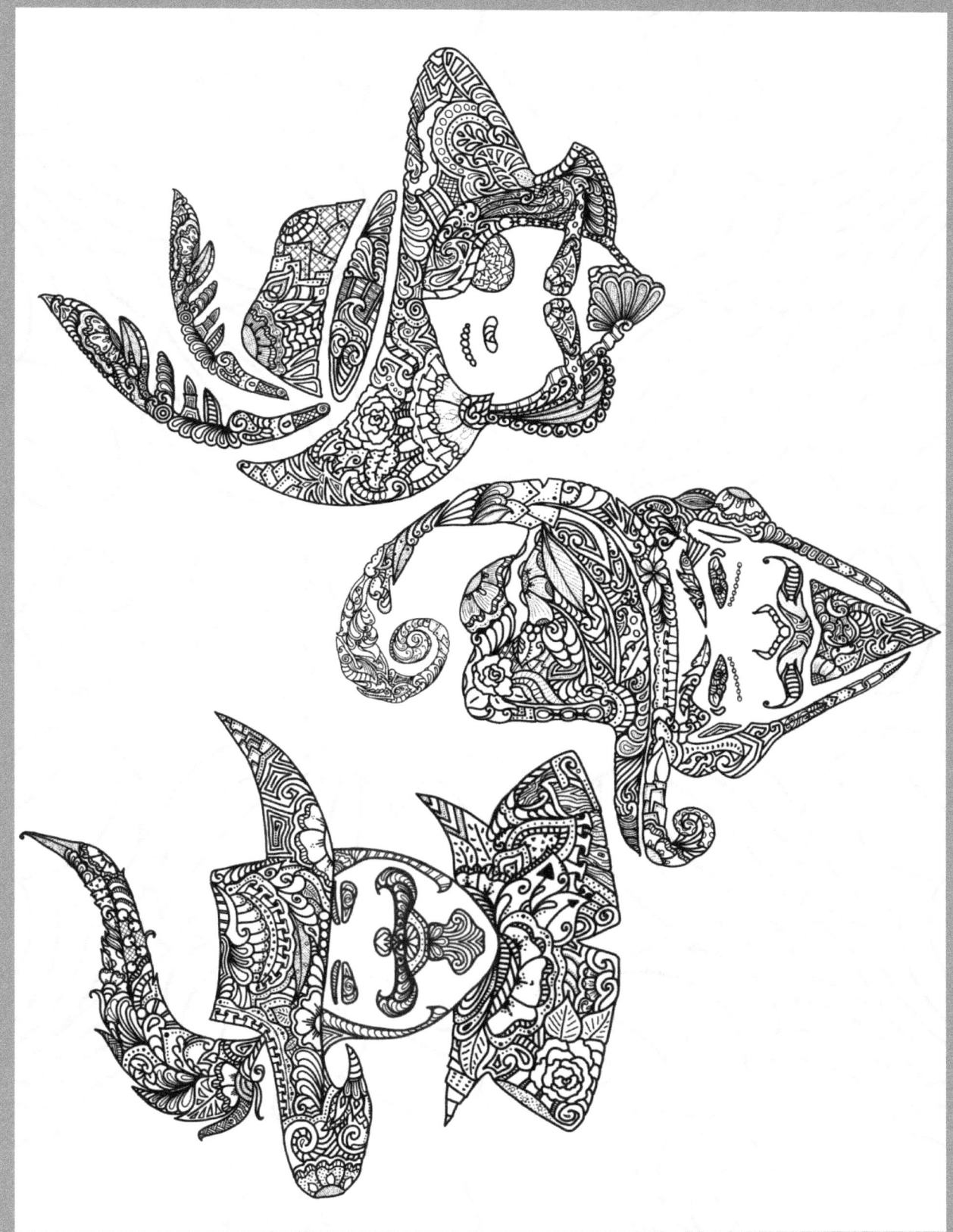

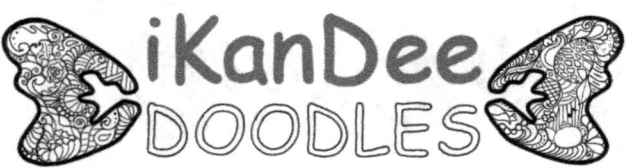

"APPLE"

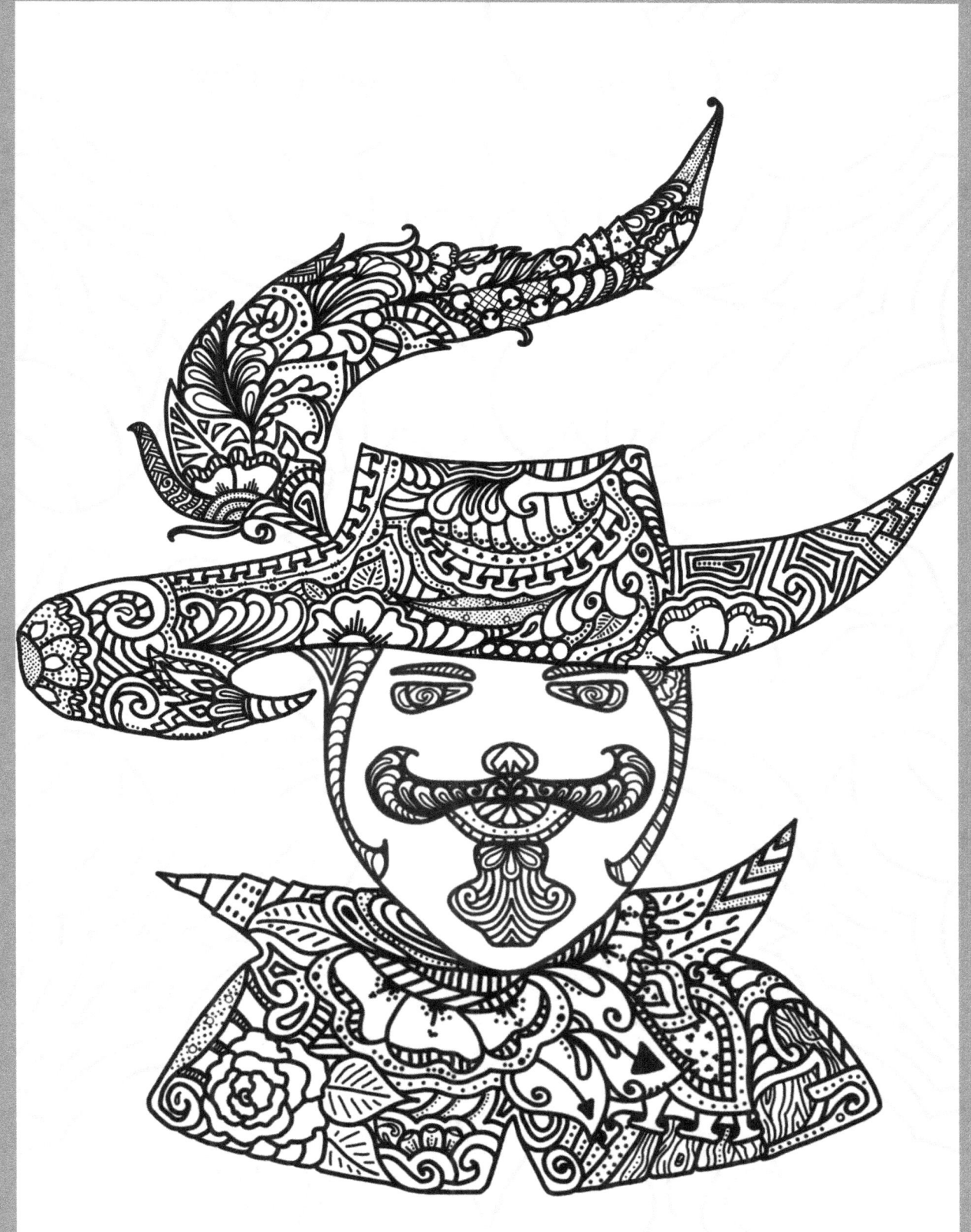

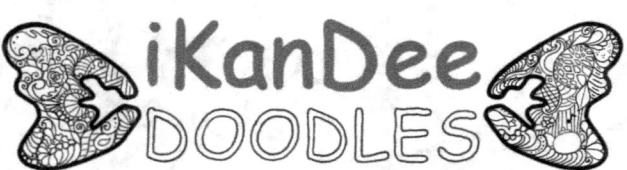

"PEACHES"

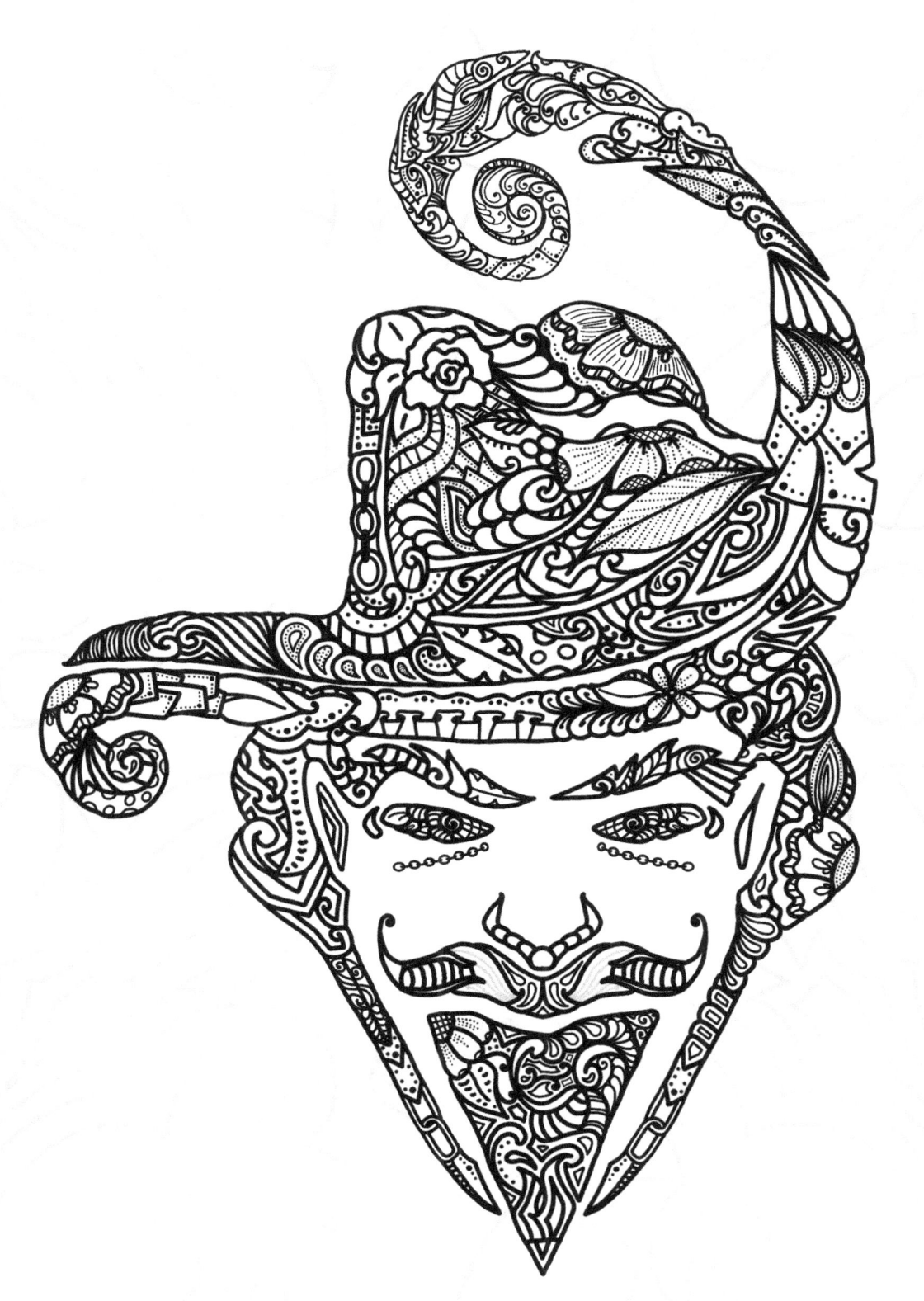

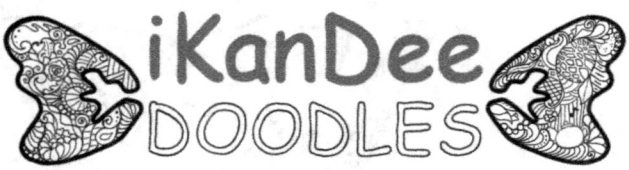

"PUMPKIN"

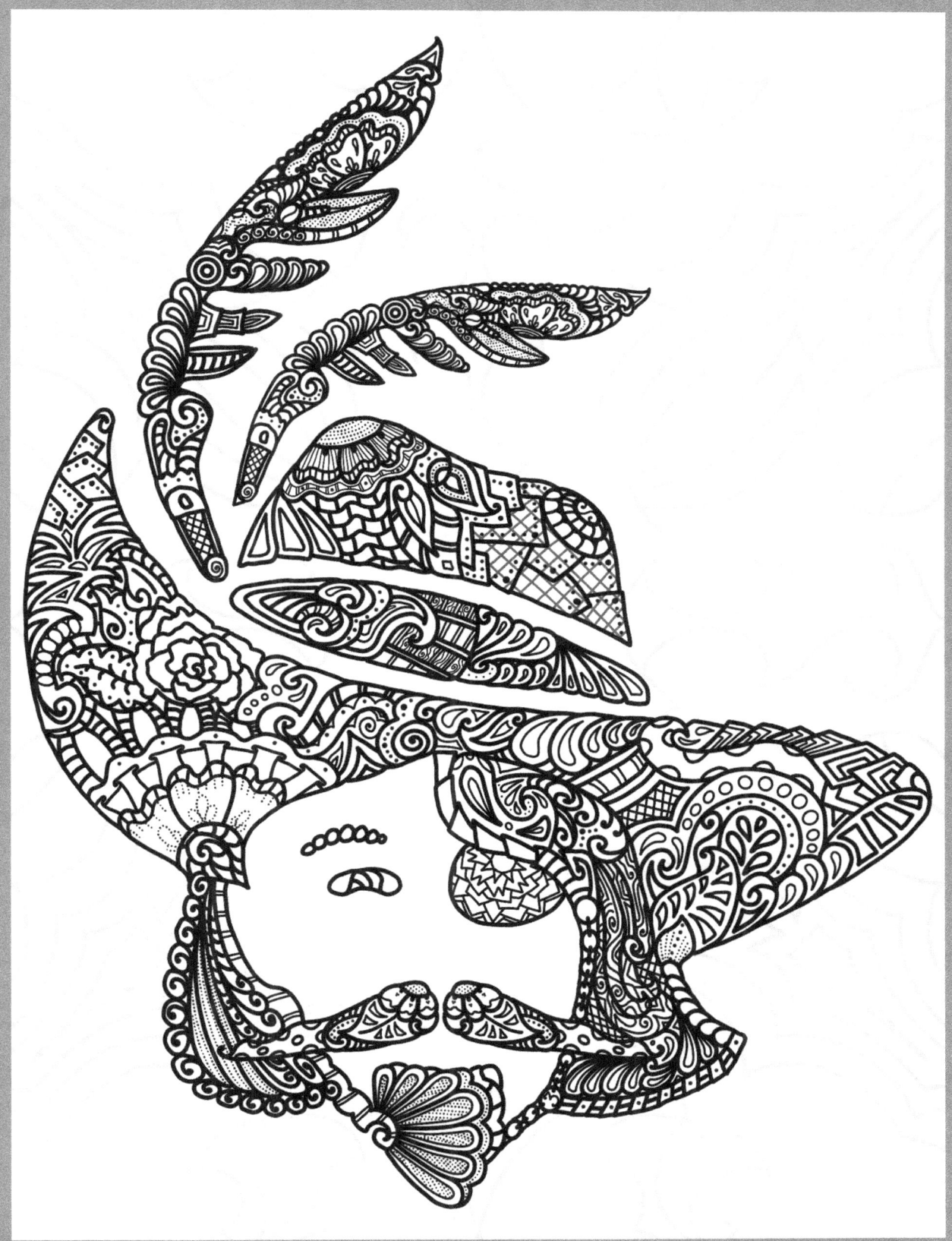

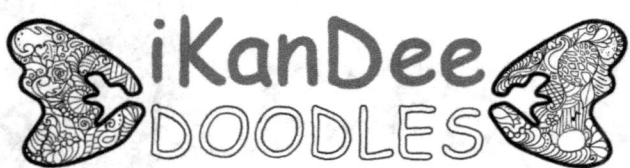

"PIE"

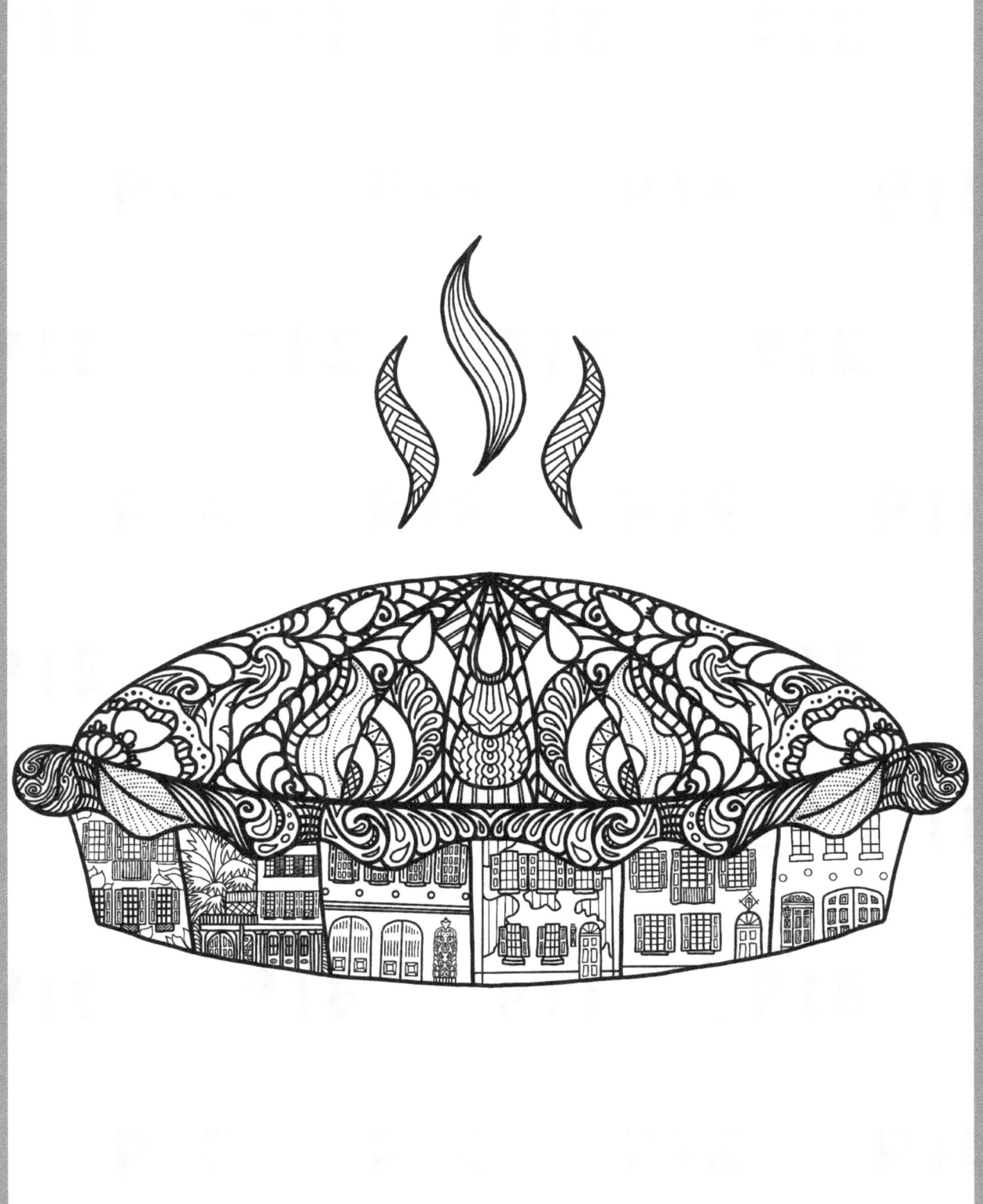

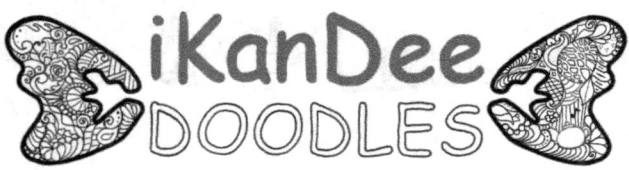

"Three Blind Mice"

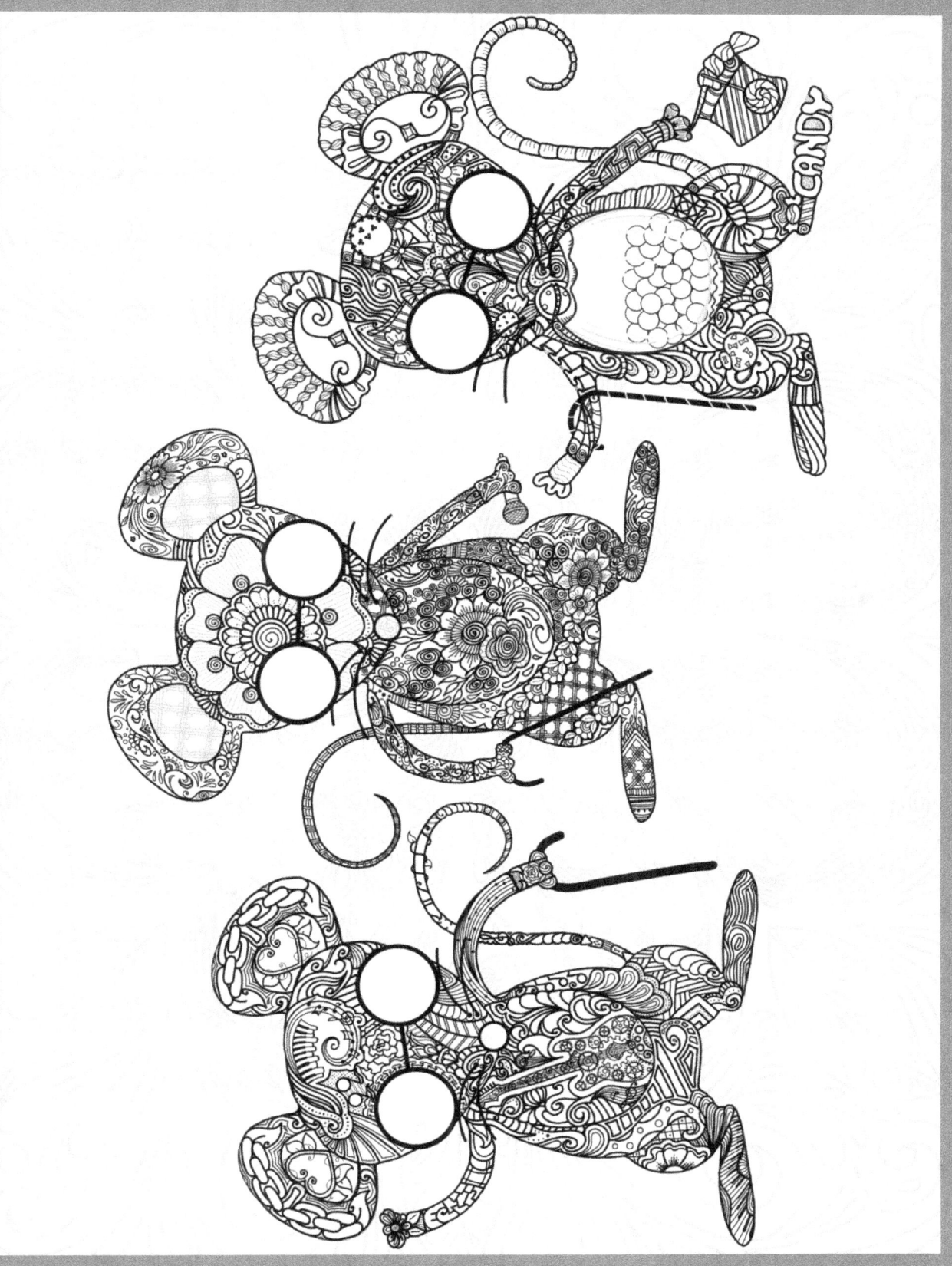

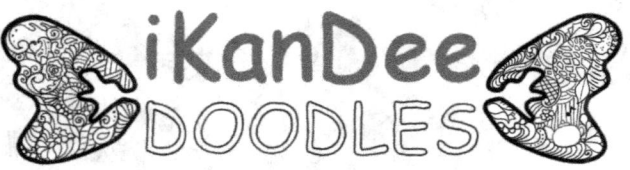

"Rock -N- Roll"

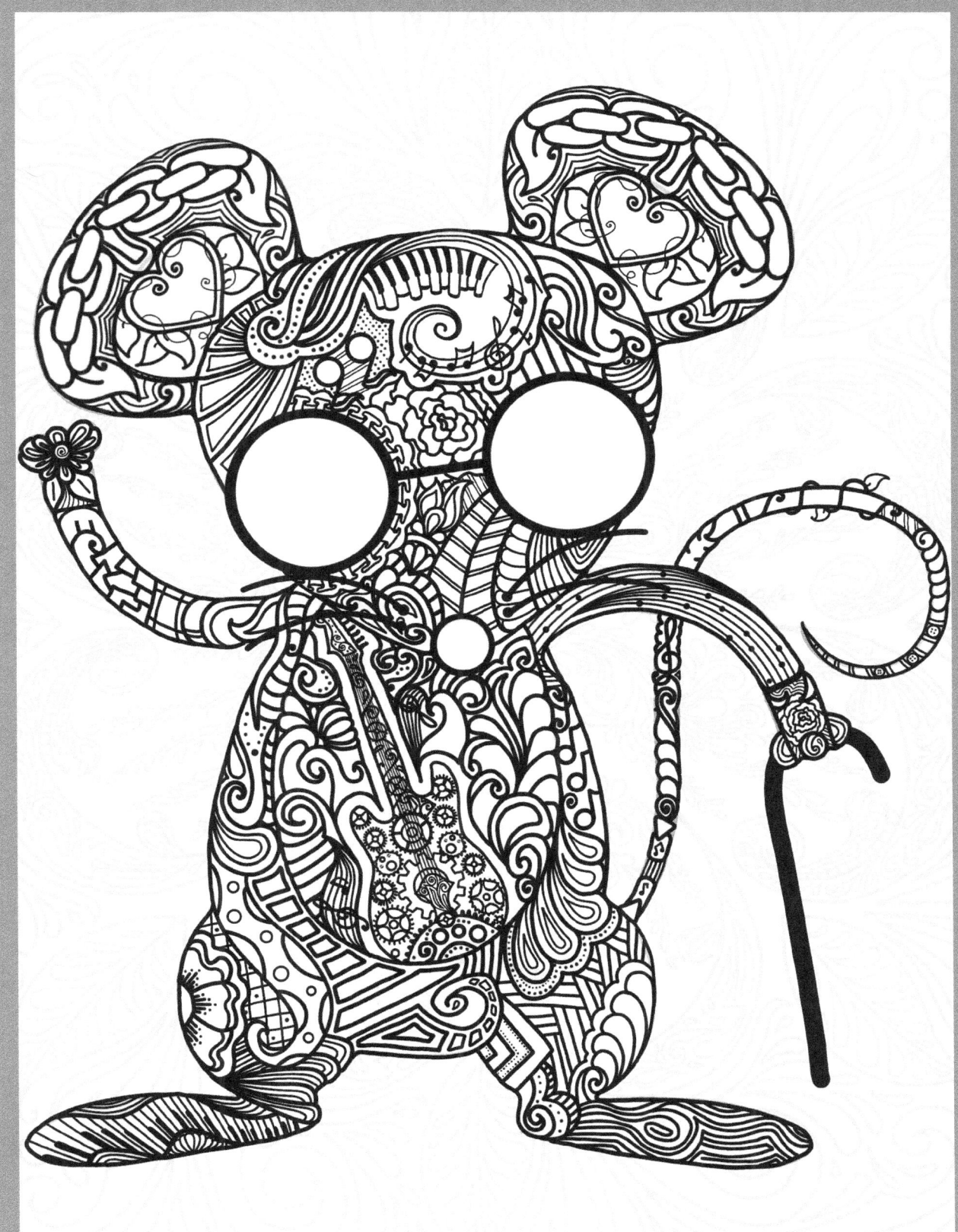

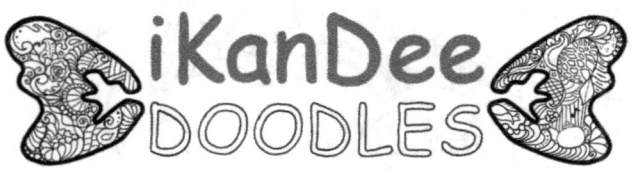

"Jelly Roll"

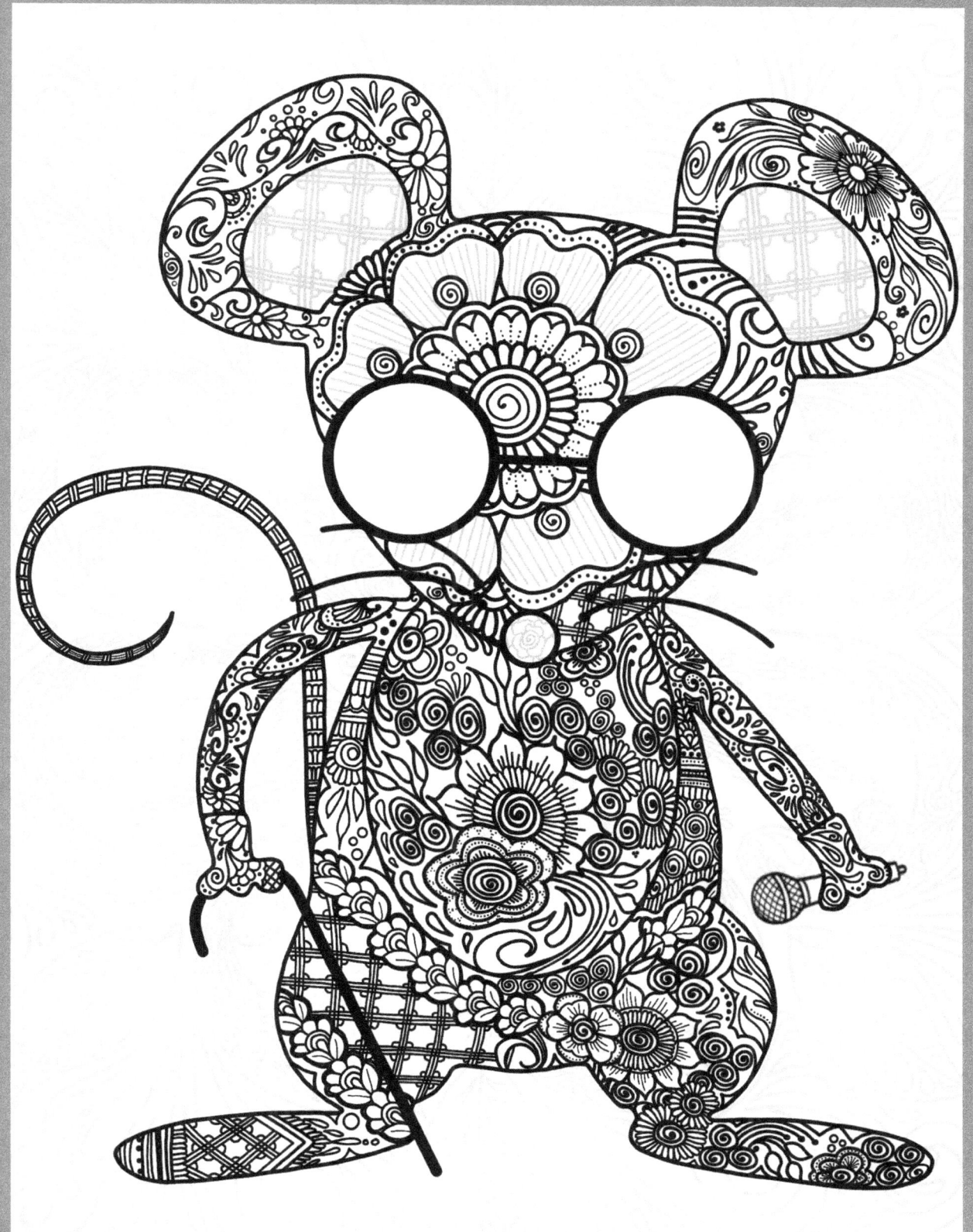

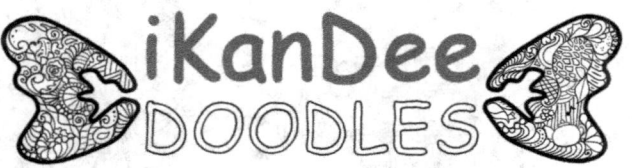

"Candy Roll"

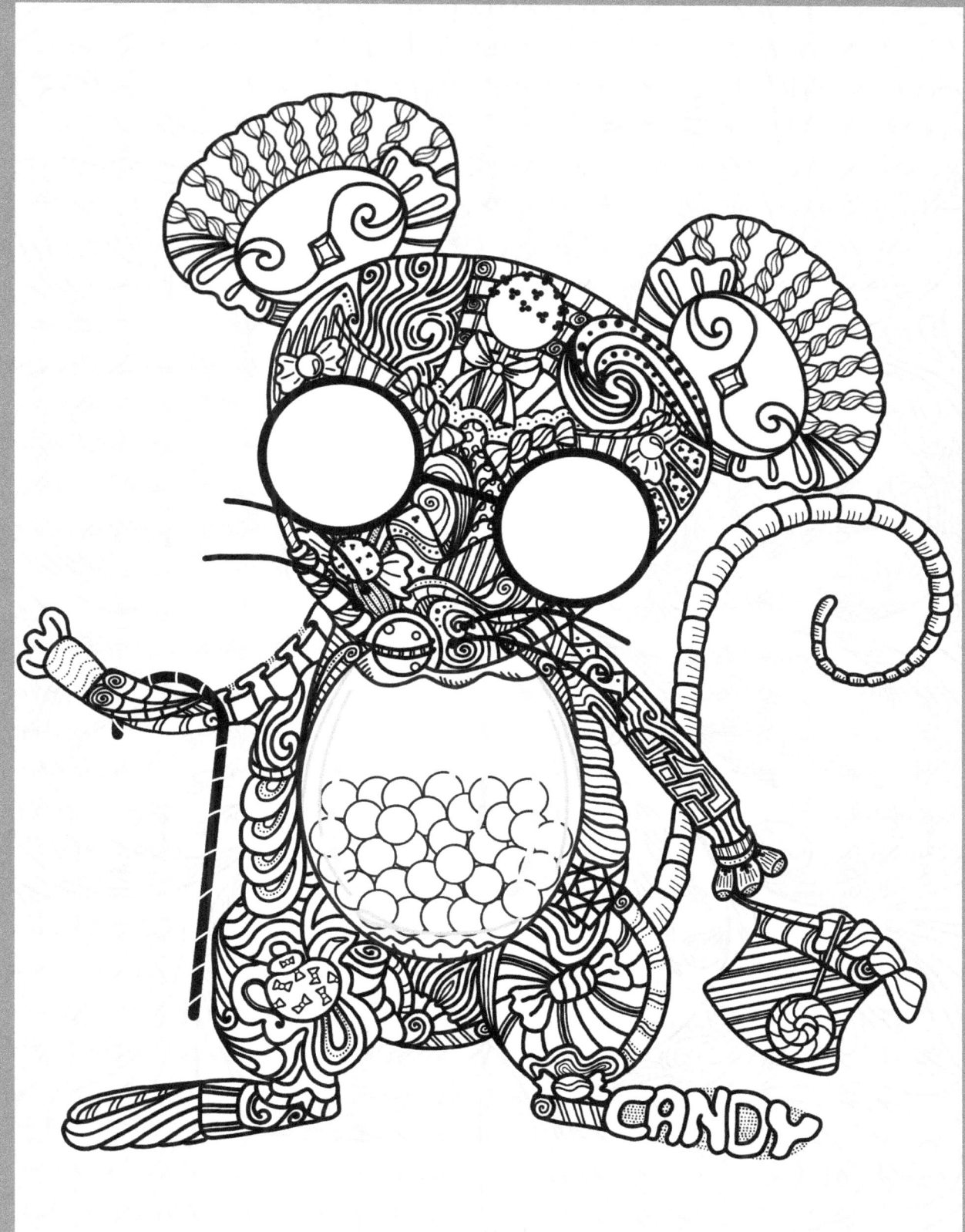

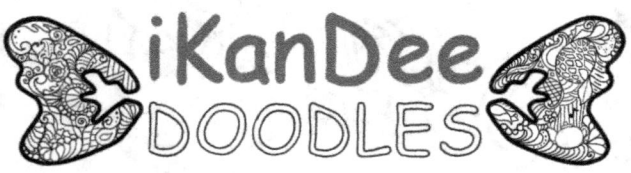

"It's Your DOODLE Page"

ABOUT THE ARTIST
"There is no normal, there's just LIFE, sew (so) get on with it"

Sheila D(ee) is a breast cancer survivor, lives with Dale, her wonderful hubby, two large dogs, JerZee & Hankford, two little dogs, Lola, a pug mix and Bella, a Yorkie. The mother of 3, mama to 5, Grammie to 12 and 5 great-grandchildren.

She is self taught at most of what she does and she considers herself somewhat of a computer nerd.

She has always been a doodler, over the last few years, her DOODLES took on new meanings, as she dealt with stress and the grief of losing loved ones...

Her hope, is that these silly iKanDee DOODLES will help you in some small measure, as they have her in creating them... : D

Side Note ~ D is her middle initial and nickname given to Sheila by her mom. She added the "(ee)" over 20 years ago, to have an online name...

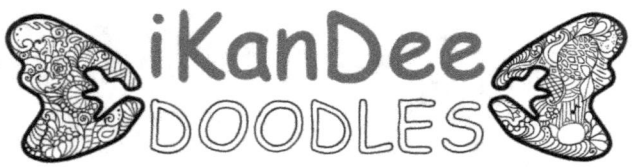

"Huggs & Smiles, D(ee)"

www.ingramcontent.com/pod-product-compliance
Lightning Source LLC
Chambersburg PA
CBHW080910220526
45466CB00011BA/3539